Shinto Temples of Sapporo, Japan

A TRAVEL PHOTO ART BOOK

LAINE CUNNINGHAM

Shinto Temples of Sapporo, Japan

A Travel Photo Art Book

Published by Sun Dogs Creations
Changing the World One Book at a Time
Print ISBN: 978-1-951389-20-8

Cover Image by Laine Cunningham
Cover Design by Angel Leya

Copyright © 2023 Laine Cunningham

All rights reserved. No part of this book may be reproduced in any form or by any means, electronic, mechanical, digital, photocopying or recording, except for the inclusion in a review, without permission in writing from the publisher.

Japanese temples are peaceful places that enshrine Shinto beliefs. Omikuji, slips of paper with fortunes people have left for the resident spirits, flutter in the breeze. On Shichi-Go-San, or Seven-Five-Three day, boys and girls don traditional outfits before visiting the shrines. Marriage ceremonies occur throughout the year, often with the couples in wedding kimonos.

The main festival of the Hokkaido Shrine is Sapporo Matsuri. A portable Shinto shrine is paraded down the streets leading onto the property. The mikoshi is thought to carry a holy spirit, so the people in the procession chant as they carry it along. At the Gokoku Shrine in Nakajima Park, water flows across the front part of the grounds. The shimenawa, or straw rope, at Yahiko Shrine sets off the entrance in grand style. The centuries-old shibakuri tree at Soma Shrine offers shade on a hill overlooking part of the city.

No matter which of these shrines you visit, the experience will stay with you long after you've returned home.

SHAVE

CITRUS

SEAM

BOLTED

PEBBLE

GREETINGS

SHOAL

TANGENT

DUSK

TUSK

ZEST

SHEEN

WAIT

STRIKE

SUNDOG

SHIVER

SHORELINE

WISHING

SCORCH

UNFOLD

SEEK

ARK

BUOY

DIP

RESERVOIR

STARK

HUM

GUIDING

OWL

STREAM

BERTH

LAP

DEN

LIGHTER

COMPOSITION

COSMIC

QUEST

FRONS

MINGLE

HUFF

TITLES IN THIS SERIES

Gardens of Sapporo, Japan
Mt. Moiwa, Sapporo, Japan
Shinto Temples of Sapporo, Japan
Shrines of Sapporo, Japan
Parks of Sapporo, Japan
Sapporo City, Japan

www.ingramcontent.com/pod-product-compliance
Lightning Source LLC
Chambersburg PA
CBHW051359110526
44592CB00023B/2882